THE MILD DAY

by William Bronk

Light and Dark (1956)
The World, the Worldless (1964)
The Empty Hands (1969)
That Tantalus (1971)
To Praise the Music (1972)
The New World (1974)
A Partial Glossary: Two Essays (1974)
Silence and Metaphor (1975)
Finding Losses (1976)
The Meantime (1976)
My Father Photographed with Friends (1976)
The Force of Desire (1979)
*The Brother in Elysium: Ideas of Friendship
         and Society in the United States* (1980)
Life Supports: New and Collected Poems (1981)
Vectors and Smoothable Curves: Collected Essays (1983)
Careless Love and Its Apostrophes (1985)
Manifest; and Furthermore (1987)
Death Is the Place (1989)
Living Instead (1991)
Some Words (1992)
The Mild Day (1993)

THE MILD DAY

poems by

WILLIAM BRONK

Talisman House, Publishers
Hoboken, New Jersey

Published in the United States of America by

       Talisman House, Publishers
       Box 1117
       Hoboken, NJ 07030

Manufactured in the United States of America

Library of Congress Cataloging-in-Publication Data

Bronk, William.
    The mild day : poems / by William Bronk
        p.   cm.
    ISBN 1-883689-01-5 (lib. bdg.) : $29.95. -- ISBN: 1-883689-00-7
(pbk.) : $9.95
    I. Title
    PS3552.R65M5   1993
    811'.54--dc20   93-5346
                                                  CIP

CONTENTS

THE MILD DAY

SAFARI

It's like going to Africa to live
with animals all around us, animals
regardless of us and we not the life
of the place ourselves as in this universe,
on earth even, forces are
that we don't see the way animals
could be seen but are around and are
regardless of us who are not the life of the place.
Awed, we stand our foreign ground. We watch.

CENTRAL CASTING

The sadnesses are just as real and the fun
is just as real—don't mistake that—
whether the actors (which is to say we,
we are the actors) whether the actors play
them on the stage or off. Roles are played.
They're only actors; it doesn't happen to them.
And people are always there to take the parts.

SHORT WALK

Awake at night, I walk in the dark of the house.
Bare feet are quiet. The rooms are undisturbed.
What else had anyone's days and nights been like?
I think, now, not any more than this.

LEFT ALONE

Left alone as it seems we often are,
we can determine parts of our lives and the lives
of some around us. More than that, we say
what the world may be, how it came about
and why. We give out truth. How great we are.

Something that doesn't mean to contravene
us, something that needn't even know we are there,
in going about its own procedures, sweeps
it all away: whatever we did or said.
Sweeps us away. We are beside the point.

No matter. Close beside. The seriousness
of desire is a voice that sings us up
and, in its singing, humbles whatever claims.

WHAT'S REAL

The what that's real is not the whats and whos
being whos and doing whats, what came
upon, but just by chance, in happening.

WHO'S THERE

We need to separate ourselves from ourselves
to be ourselves. All that pain and power:
that isn't us. All that busyness,
the alienation and hate, those love affairs.

SOSTENUTO

The people in stories linger a long while
after the ones they edited from are gone.
We try to work us into a story book
even as someone other than ourselves
and life other than life, it too should last.

EASY VIRTUE

Rectitude has little to offer but one
is safe from virtue there. Virtue is hard;
it's found if ever, deviously, surprised.

VERBAL

A person is like the scene the person sees:
just there and seen to be there.
It is not the name given or the name made.
To be is the verb to be. The noun pretends.

THE SEEING EYE

The lives we live have little to do with our life
which watches those performances as those
of someone else it doesn't need. It needs
nothing; it has us it doesn't need.
It lets us, though, see wonders through its eye.

GOOD STORY

Stories aren't only to ease us into sleep
but, even more to rock us awake easy:
god stories,
science stories,
all because
know isn't.

SUBJECT MATTER

This writing is pencil marks easily
erased from paper which, itself, will fall
apart as its writer will. It means to note
whatever doesn't depend on any note
or record the writer needs to make of it.

ON OUR OWN

Life doesn't much trust us; it keeps a lot to itself.
Expected at parties, it may send someone else
and day to day it doesn't show up on a job.
We're on our own. In disasters and wars it has
a foxhole to be safe in while thousands of us
are wiped—or wipe each other—out. Long years
can go away with merely a glimpse of it.
Sometimes in bed, it stays with me all night.

WASTREL

Life-wasted life-stuff like
leaves yearly, fossils once, we'll
lie wasted,
wasted by
that which
waste isn't,
life is,
is life.

THE DRAWING

Art's care
discriminates
not art
not life
but art's desire
and life sees
itself there
and is drawn.

THE JUNCTURE

In great distances, our measured
becomes immeasurable. You needn't go far
to find the place. There's where you are.

THE SWITCHYARD

The things we think about we think about
in different terms one and another time.
The switch is easy; it's not as though we know
about what things are there outside the mind.

STORY TIME

Truth doesn't trouble us and we
don't trouble truth. What confronts what once
we believed is other belief coming on.

SIMPLY STATED

People is all we are. Whatever we do
to one another or what is done to us,
things go back to what they were all along.
It's even as though something of us survive
our annihilation, something of us were real.

DISCRETIONARY

What you look at then and now may be
the same though what you see is not. In sleep,
we can recognize people we know
and places from times awake. It's a different sight.
We hadn't known. It's not that we were wrong
in either case. It's just that asleep, awake,
what other times, we never see what is.

INDICATIVE

I, the inanimate, marked for discard,
watch, in me, that life whom I attend.
How it flourishes in me its husk!
If life were no longer life, life still will be.

THE SAYER

That life that says me poems says other things
to other men and other times than this.
It says those times. It doesn't say itself.

EMPOWERMENT

Even up and moving mornings I may
be yet to be born still, still in the dark
swell. Life is a power apart there,
no power of mine. It peoples me.
Life will be that power when it seems I am.

UNCREATION

Lions for example, would you have had lions?
                                        Or skunks
would you?
                At inconceivable distances, stars?
What function could you think of for us?
                                        None
of this was made. Ever. All of it there.

ON OR OFF THE FIELD

Maybe in congress or combat it's not
possible to deal with issues we think
to deal with.
              Life contends with itself
without us.
              Instead, we game in stadia
in symbols as if to win or lose our lives.

FAITHFUL REPLICA

We make a replica of our belief
and there, as fact, it is. A rough job
but look at it there. We must have been right all along.
Time passes. Euphoria awhile.

DIVIDERS

As of us or the world, experience can't be explained.
But we give names to it and, by common consent,
we make familiars of the strange. *Us*
and the *world* are kinds of discretions we make by our names,
maps where the mind can measure in the mapless mind.
And we divide and divide trying for ultimates.
All is the only ultimate. All
is the unexplained. As of us and the world.

SPADES, KETTLES AND ANONYMITY

Each separate entity anywhere had its own
proper name I needed only to find
or learn from other's findings.
                              Now I know
their names are pin-ons we give to them and give
ourselves, that separation is not the truth
and much won't be named even with made-up names.

THE FIELD

Are there some gravities of ordered thought
that orbit us around a sun the way
our floating earth is orbited?
                              Our feet
are on the ground but nothing unders the mind
to give us who or why we are or what
that sun might be.
                        Desire alone attracts
us together to make a common sense and found
an unfounded order, a house of thought to leave
unlived and empty almost as soon as built.

MISCALLING

Everyday things—work, people—in fact
are real. We sometimes ask if they are. They are.
They're not what we call them though but something else
and not such that we can ever know.

MAIN FRAME

The enormous intricacy of detail and the
design elements built into each
not only of us but of all animal
and plant examples is what distracts and misleads
us, even as its discovery delights
us. In its extravagant waste there doesn't seem
a need for any of it. We look for the use
or direction as though it should be in all of this.
The intention, if there is one, is not there.

NON-SPATIAL

We meet life in the living and in us too.
It walks in and looks around and leaves.
We aren't life. It doesn't need the space.

IMPOVERISHMENT

Poverty vowed is, for the worshiper,
indifferent virtue. It doesn't count for him.
But the what worshiped has to have and to be
entire nothing, whole impoverishment:
an undiscoverable bubble in the worshiper's blood
or a big bubble he lives in, its film unseen.

THE WAY IT WORKS

The material world is a way—otherwise
difficult, even impossible—
to speak about something that may be.
The material world makes it more real to us,
is an emblem, a kind of metaphor, we can put
our hands on and manipulate. We have
the big bang to bring the thing about
but everything is there before that.
It has to be. And aren't we too?

SPEECHES

Words change shape and come to have
other meanings in other languages.
How do we know the unspoken stays the same?

OUTSIDE

Awake, but early. ENTRANCE is where I've been brought.
I know I can't go in. Dark yet.
I could get up and turn away. I stay.

ADVERSE POSSESSION

The twisted anguishes of loss and the wild
releases of elation aren't given to us
by life. Life doesn't know or care we are.
Only our own declaration lays
a blame there and makes a claim on life.

HOW WE HANDLE PRACTICAL MATTERS

In the real world of practicality
there are no real problems. It is understood
that symbolically is the only possible
way to deal with the real impossible.

TRANSACTIONS

Transactions kept us busy. In the days and weeks
of being here we wanted to do what we could:
buying and selling, of course, but straightening out
organization and looking for what could come.
And there was interaction, getting to know
the people, making friends and more than friends.
We did all that. And we studied the area.
It was an active life; we thought it was.
You may not notice the traces. I could point them out.

LOVE'S AVERMENT

My sure desire is a covering canopy
and, under it, I stand secure in want
of some security known not to be.
Desire wants uncaring what isn't there.

TERMINOLOGY

Except in its own terms everything
is too tiny ever even to be seen.
This applies to distant galaxies
and as well to microscopics closer by.
Much has to be in our terms for us
to see it: stars we name, our own selves
and other people, furniture in rooms
of houses, familiar things to make a world
familiar with us.
                But we see enough beyond
it to know that, beyond our terms, our terms are too
tiny to be seen in a place anywhere,
and like the functions of arithmetic
can ground on no support outside themselves.

ENCOUNTER

Jolted by a face up close on the street
because close it was unknowable
I remembered to know that's how we all are.

SUBVERSIVES

We needn't try to keep it secret from life
—we flash it in life's face—and life doesn't care
what we do and wouldn't see it anyway.
But we, as people, are an underground in life's worlds
wanting another world, a world of ours.
We conspire stories to tell about that world.

DEFLATION

The way the night dream deflates on its own
in the morning's lighted air, its absolutes
of mass and power gone, is the same way
those things of mornings and days, solid things
we kept to have—the real engagements, the fun—
deflate too as we age. And the people, the people. . .

TOKEN

Even my father, dead some fifty years
and buried away, dreamed back one night and we
were easy and laughing together though never before.

THE CONFLAGRATION

That fire in Alexandria that burnt
the books: the books were never written again.
People alive then died and the ones
to remember them died. People came afterwards
and still come. There still are lots of books.
Loss is more than any values they have.

ACTS OF DEVOTION

Devotion's fact is realer than its truth.

We look for a shape for our desire which has
no shape.
        How beautiful they are, those shapes
desire makes for itself.
            And how they praise
the beauty of our desire when it has their shape.

We could lie in them forever if their praise were true.

NOT YES NOR NO

Inside the axioms believed, there are
consistencies and these consistencies
demonstrable. But truth? Truth we can't
even formulate to begin to say.
Nothing we can prove or deny is truth.

MORNING

I wake hard-grasped, quivered alive
in what I can't recover. I want to go back.
But it's time to move bemused in the mild day.

BARE BOARDS AT THE GLOBE

No more than we is the rest of the natural world
life either. We love us as though we were.
The deep earth and the even deeper sky
are sets not used on life's stage.
Actors and actresses aren't seen or heard.
Sit witness of life's power. We attend.

William Bronk was born in 1918 in Hudson Falls, New York, where he currently lives. His essays are collected in *Vectors and Smoothable Curves*. His collected poems, *Life Supports*, received the American Book Award. In the words of the poet Michael Heller, Bronk "is one of our modern masters."

Designed by
Samuel Retsov

•

Text: 10 pt Garamond

•

acid-free paper

•

Printed by
McNaughton & Gunn, Inc.

ACP-8925   5/3/95

PS
3552
RG5
M5
1993